Words I Love

Words I Love

An Earthly/Heavenly Romance

VOLUME 5

Charles Santiago

RESOURCE *Publications* • Eugene, Oregon

WORDS I LOVE
An Earthly/Heavenly Romance, Volume 5

Copyright © 2025 Charles Santiago. All rights reserved. Except for brief quotations in critical publications or reviews, no part of this book may be reproduced in any manner without prior written permission from the publisher. Write: Permissions, Wipf and Stock Publishers, 199 W. 8th Ave., Suite 3, Eugene, OR 97401.

Resource Publications
An Imprint of Wipf and Stock Publishers
199 W. 8th Ave., Suite 3
Eugene, OR 97401

www.wipfandstock.com

PAPERBACK ISBN: 979-8-3852-5133-9
HARDCOVER ISBN: 979-8-3852-5134-6
EBOOK ISBN: 979-8-3852-5135-3

VERSION NUMBER 042925

Contents

Introduction | ix

1. While We Rendezvous | 3
2. Before the Dawn | 4
3. A Temple | 5
4. Neither Dead nor Gone | 6
5. I Will Find You | 7
6. Adam and Eve | 8
7. I Can Do a Lot | 9
8. Chant, My Dear | 10
9. Fly with the Wind | 11
10. This Was *Meant* to Be! | 12
11. Two Worlds, We've Spanned! | 13
12. Do Not Rant and Rave! | 14
13. *Our Maker* Joined Us | 15
14. This Secret Place | 16
15. We Grow Closer | 17
16. Peace and Joy and Love | 18
17. Today and Yesterday | 19
18. Especially at Three | 20
19. Sealed | 21
20. The Other Me | 22
21. Feel Our Union | 23
22. A Gift | 24
23. More and More, It's Clear | 25
24. Earthly/Heavenly Bliss | 26
25. Heaven's Sway | 27
26. I Confess to Know | 28

27. Prove, to Me, You Fear No Dread | 29
28. Another World | 30
29. Traveling | 31
30. Like Two Swans | 32
31. Years and Years Ago | 33
32. Speechless | 34
33. Our Special Zone | 35
34. Love Abounds | 36
35. Romantic Movies | 37
36. Wedding Bells Are Ringing | 38
37. Via Highway 27 | 40
38. There's a Lot That I Can Do! | 41
39. Death Is Not a Separation! | 42
40. A Clever Rhyme | 43
41. Our Mortal Scar | 44
42. I Believe in Resurrection! | 45
43. So Much More than Clay! | 47
44. Harmonize with Me | 49
45. These Words You Love | 50
46. Laugh, My Earthly Man! | 51
47. We Taught Death How to Behave | 52
48. A Higher Way | 53
49. Month by Month | 54
50. Walking in Eternity | 55
51. Soon Enough | 56
52. Two Temples | 57
53. We Adhere | 58
54. Our Union | 59
55. Our Special Time | 60
56. Reach for Heaven | 61
57. Come Aboard! | 62
58. Let Me Know You See | 63
59. I'm Beside You | 64
60. This Special Life | 65
61. Quite a Love Affair! | 66
62. Row Your Boat | 67

63. Just a Scar | 68
64. A New Creation | 69
65. *Read* These Words! | 70
66. All Is Well | 71
67. Fly! | 72
68. Wicked Earthly Eyes | 73
69. Our Life's Not Through! | 74
70. Here, Below | 75
71. I'm Trailing You! | 76
72. Increase Awareness | 77
73. Joined Today, *As One* | 78
74. *Happy,* Be! | 79
75. An Earthly/Heavenly Mystery | 80
76. *Bodies,* We Don't Need | 81
77. Heaven's Lovely Glow | 82
78. When *You* Embraced Me | 83
79. This Love Affair | 84
80. Just a Passing Phase | 85
81. By Our Maker, We Are Known | 86
82. A Sun Beyond | 87
83. Clasp My Hand | 88
84. To Love, *Today* | 89
85. Without or With | 90
86. Every Single Day | 91
87. Every Moment of the Day | 92
88. Thank the Angels! | 93
89. *Dead and Gone* Is *So* Untrue! | 94
90. A Lovely Mystery | 95
91. Because We Are a Unity | 96
92. This Holy Hush | 97
93. Death Tried Hard! | 98
94. Every Moment | 99
95. *Stronger,* Grows Our Love | 100
96. A Doorway | 101
97. I *Remember* You | 102
98. Yearning for Our Liberty | 103

99. A World Apart | 104
100. Love That Never Dies! | 105
101. Lovers Thrill to Unity! | 106
102. Abiding in Our Unity | 107
103. Timbuktu, O Timbuktu! | 108
104. Let's Meet at End of Day | 109
105. I Believed | 110
106. Graves and Tombs and Pyres, and Such | 111
107. Earthly/Heavenly Ecstasy | 112
108. Love Has Saved Us | 113
109. ABCs | 114
110. All We Need | 115
111. Believe in Love | 116
112. Our Bold Romance | 117
113. Resurrection Love | 118
114. Going Our Way | 119
115. "It" | 120
116. *Today,* We Live! | 121
117. This Life of Liberty | 122
118. I'm Content | 123
119. We Still Are *One!* | 124
120. When It's Time | 125

Introduction

My wife died on July 27, 2019. It intrigues me to think about what my life, since then, would have been like without the appearance of "our lovely creed" ("the creed, *by death,* we came to heed"). What would have occupied my time for all the many, many hours that have been spent writing and reading over 2,500 poems? What would my spiritual development have been like without the tremendous impact on my life of that lovely creed? What kind of man would I be today without that creed? I *wonder.*

Some might think it was all a big mistake—a misunderstanding on my part, not being aware of the fact that I was supposed to "get on with my life." I could understand that way of thinking if I believed in "dead and gone." I *don't* believe in "dead and gone." But I *did* believe in "dead and gone" when my wife died in my arms.

Our lovely creed is a reflection of what happened to me (to us) after my wife died. I came to understand that my wife's death was our second wedding! It *does* seem strange that a man would attend his own wedding and not realize it was a wedding until *after the fact*. It certainly wasn't like that at our first wedding. But this second wedding was a wedding between a heavenly bride and her earthly groom. It took a while for the earthly groom to wake up to the fact that he got hitched again!

I became aware that my wife was communicating with me without words, without touch. It was a communication that I felt spiritually and through the circumstances of my daily life. In a way (but not *really*), I think I could have missed the heavenly cues, and continued living, as a pawn of Mr. Dead and Gone. Thank heavens, "dead and gone" was replaced by "alive and here!"

Introduction

But, it has not been easy. Though I reject the idea of "dead and gone" as regards my wife—and in spite of indescribable experiences of continued union—it seems like there is a switch within me that is set, as a default setting, on the position of "dead and gone." My battle against Mr. Dead and Gone is, ultimately, resolved in complete victory. But I find that I must engage him in battle very frequently. He is very crafty and very persistent! Writing, reading, understanding, and assimilating the ideas expressed in our lovely creed, are the perfect antidote to Mr. Dead and Gone's obnoxious assaults upon our earthly/heavenly contentment. Our earthly/heavenly communion is a growing, ever-present reality but, at the same time, it involves struggle—this "lovely war."

This lovely war will culminate in yet another wedding—wedding number three. Wearing each other, we will walk down the aisle once more.

Poems

1. While We Rendezvous, 1/31/25

A morning poem

It's JUST the BODY, dear, that died.
I am here, with you, today.
I'M your everlasting bride—
BY your SIDE, dear, come what may.
In your dreams, I'll speak to you,
All throughout our rendezvous.
WE can feel this love of ours,
In daylight and in nighttime hours.

WHILE we rendezvous, my love,
There's ANOTHER rendezvous!
Angels, in the heavens, above,
Rendezvous with ME AND YOU!
This love is more than YOU AND ME—
It's PART of HEAVEN'S mystery.
Learn to trust the angels, dear,
Guiding us through month and year.

Day by day, we find it's TRUE—
YES, death WAS our entranceway
To life, again, for me and you,
In and out of night and day.
Now, beloved, Earthly beau,
Rise, to live that life below.
Heaven smiles on you and me,
Granting us this unity!

2. Before the Dawn

Charles Santiago, 1/31/25
Inspired by music of Marc Enfroy, "Before the Dawn"

Oh, my dear, how beautiful, this life!
I'm *entranced* by *you,* and *you alone.*
I'm in awe that you're my wife—
In awe, my dear, of *how* we've *grown!*
Can it be, we'll live again—
Again, beyond a mere Earth span?
Yes, dear, you and I will soar—
Other lovely worlds, to explore.

I'm in awe of how we live,
Entwined forever and ever, my dear.
A *greater* love, this love can give,
A love beyond this world, down here.
Eternity found you and me,
And sealed us as a unity.
A greater love, dear, a *greater love*
Sweeps us up to worlds above!

I'm in awe of what we are,
One with all creation, dear!
We can *feel,* from here, afar,
A distant, wondrous atmosphere—
A place, my dear, we're headed to,
A place that's meant for me and you.
Before the dawn, awake with me,
And let us greet eternity!

3. A Temple, 2/1/25

I direct my **thoughts** to you,
And, *when* I *do,* I *find* it's *true—*
There's no *need* to grieve, my love.
We're *living in* our home above.

Dear, I think of you and find,
Soul to soul, are WE entwined.
THERE'S no NEED, my dear, to think
GOD does NOT provide a link.

Our link, my dear, is *all my life,*
Preserving us, as man and wife.
As I *live* down here, below,
I can *feel* your heav'nly glow.

We LIVE, above. We LIVE, below—
A heav'nly belle and Earthly beau.
Angels guide us on our way
THOUGH you're ROBED, dear, STILL, in CLAY.

I'm so *glad* we've *found* this *way*
Though I'm *robed,* dear, *still,* in *clay.*
In *all* the *things* I do, down here,
I can *feel* that *you* are *near.*

Remember THIS, dear Earthly beau—
You're A TEMPLE, there, below.
In all those Earthly things you do,
I'M residing, dear, IN YOU.

4. Neither Dead nor Gone, 2/1/25

A séance poem

"Bumblebee, bumblebee"—
The name, my dear, you gave to me.
A bumblebee, I love to be,
Rejoicing in our unity.

"Bumblebee," I call you, dear,
To help you triumph over fear—
Fear that I would disappear—
Fear that I AM GONE, "up here."

Neither dead nor gone, are *you*.
Well, my dear, I *know* it's *true!*
I *know* it's *true*. I *really do*—
Because, my dear, *we rendezvous!*

I can see, our rhymes, you've read;
For, YOU have GOT it THROUGH your HEAD,
The reason there's no cause for dread
Is RESURRECTION FROM THE DEAD!

5. I Will Find You, 2/2/25

Faithful to those words, "I do,"
*I am **living**, now, **in you.***
YOU believe these words are true—
And, so, my dear, we rendezvous!

Faithful to those words, "I do,"
I *sit* with *you*, dear, *in* our *pew*.
Oh, my darling, *what a view*,
Far surpassing Timbuktu!

*I will **find** you, bumblebee,*
AGAIN and AGAIN. Just WAIT—*You'll SEE.*
WE have GAINED our liberty—
We CAN'T ESCAPE our unity!

I will **wait**, dear—*You* will **see**—
Till *Earth* days *are* all *through* with *me.*
I will **wait**, my dear, for thee,
Until our wedding number three!

6. Adam and Eve

Charles Santiago, 2/2/25

I am *fine,* dear. *I* am *fine.*
More than *that,* dear—I'm *divine.*
A holy temple, I've become,
Drunk, my dear, with heav'nly rum!
When I *feel* you, deep inside,
Up, in heaven, I abide.
Abide in me, and I, in you,
There—and *here,* in Timbuktu.
This love we share—What *can* I *say?*
It *lifts* me *out* of night and day.
This sweet communion that we share
Is almost more than I can bear!
I must *leave,* dear. *I* must *leave,*
To live, above, with you, my Eve.
Adam's spirit *must* ascend,
To meet with Eve, beyond the bend.
Let us tend a garden, dear,
Far above this life down here!

7. I Can Do a Lot, 2/2/25

Consider, MY dear BUMBLEBEE,
That, YES, you ARE the OTHER ME.
LIVE that LIFE down THERE, below—
Hand in hand, we still can go.
Do you think I'm unconcerned?
Do you think, our life, I've spurned?
Of COURSE not, MY dear EARTHLY BEAU!
OF our LOVE, up here, I crow:
"My EARTHLYL BEAU has FAITH that WE
Can, STILL, a loving couple, be.
Death, he knows, is Eden's snake,
Who never could, our union, break."
Consider me, dear, BY your SIDE
Ever since my body died.
Even in your leisure hours,
WE are LINKED by heav'nly powers.
ALL does NOT DEPEND on YOU!
TWO, it takes, to rendezvous!
*I can do a **lot**, my love,*
To help you see our home, above!

8. Chant, My Dear, 2/3/25

Signs are leading me, my dear,
To our *lovely,* heav'nly home.
Earthly worries disappear—
We unite and *chant,* dear, "*Om.*"
Two *worlds* are *spanned,* I *understand,*
Because of love's demand.

Love demands, dear heav'nly bride—
Love demands of you and me—
A *life* that's *lived,* dear, *side* by *side,*
In sweet tranquility.
Tranquility is ours, my love,
Down *here,* and *there, above.*

*Chant, my dear, "I **know** she's **here!**"*
It THRILLS me TO my CORE!
ONE, we ARE, today, my dear,
On HEAVEN'S lovely shore.
Holy Rhapsodies, we share,
BECAUSE, my dear, WE DARE!

9. Fly with the Wind, 2/4/25

Tallahassee National Cemetery, Section 4, Site 5

The wind is blowing, dear Earthly beau,
Blowing for you and me, below.
AS your FRIEND has said to you,
"Fly with the wind"—To TRUTH, be true!

Fly with the wind and come to me.
The truth, my dear, has set you free—
Free to leave your corpse, below—
Free, UP HERE, my dear, to glow.

Let that wind that blows, below,
BRING you up HERE, dear Earthly beau.
"Fly with the wind," your friend has said.
Depart that land of mortal dread.

YOU can FLY—It's true, my dear,
Beyond that world of month and year.
The wind is blowing, down there, below.
Fly with the wind, UP HERE, to glow!

10. This Was *Meant* to Be! 2/4/25

Highway 27 rest stop north of Perry, Florida

This was *meant* to be, my dear.
This was *meant* to be!
Our union didn't disappear.
Still, we live, as *You and Me!*
Death was just an entranceway
To *heaven,* where we *live* today.

In heaven, where we live today,
Beyond the Earth, below,
Bumblebee, what CAN we SAY?
WE are NOT our BODIES—NO!
***Spirits,** dear, are **you** and **I**,*
Walking in the by-and-by!

LET that corpse, dear, find its way
TO a LONELY GRAVE.
Darling, YOU are MORE than CLAY—
LIKE an ANGEL, dear, behave!
This was MEANT to be, dear beau.
WE can travel to and fro!

11. Two Worlds, We've Spanned! 2/5/25

What a *fair* and lovely land
We have *found*, my heav'nly belle!
Two *different* worlds, we, now, have spanned.
All is well, dear. All is well.
We can walk through night and day,
A heav'nly belle and man of clay.
We can meet beyond the sun,
For, ***you*** and ***I***, my dear, are ***one***.

Two *worlds,* we've spanned. Two *worlds,* we've spanned!
Death turned out to be a friend!
He *took* us *both*, dear, by the hand,
To show, our union, cannot end.
"*Walk* with *me*. I'll *walk* with *you*" —
We have *proved*, my dear, is true!
Soul mates, darling, always find
How to *skirt* the mortal bind.

Side by side, is how we live,
Up, above, and down, below.
God, this life, can SURELY give
To you and me, my Earthly beau.
WHEN we GO for rides on Earth,
WE are sharing heav'nly mirth.
Two WORLDS, we've SPANNED, dear bumblebee,
For, God maintains our unity.

12. Do Not Rant and Rave! 2/6/25

THIS will turn out RIGHT, my love—
This problem, gnawing deep within.
Trust in mercy from above.
To worry SO, is like a sin!
Peace, my dear, is ours, to share,
Even all the way down there.
Keep your eyes, dear, on the prize—
Peace transcending Earthly skies.

Start the car and go with me
ON a RIDE to heaven's shore.
Glory in our unity
Beyond the Earth's obnoxious roar.
What on Earth could rob our peace?
Darling, from your worries, cease!
In the end, that life, below,
MUST give way to heaven's glow.

Heaven's glow, enjoy, with me,
NOW, my anxious, Earthly beau!
Abandon, dear, your misery.
Why be troubled there, below?
Remember ALL that WE have SHARED
SINCE our flesh became unpaired.
Sweetheart, do not rant and rave—
Like a HEAV'NLY beau, behave!

13. *Our Maker* Joined Us, 2/6/25

Earthly life is done, my dear!
I can ***tell,*** for ***you*** are ***here.***
It's *just* a *corpse* that holds me down,
Trying to topple my heav'nly crown.

I descended to the tomb—
Descended, dear, your Earthly groom.
But *I* was ***raised*** to heav'nly life
Because of *you*, my heav'nly wife!

Heaven knows, dear, *we* are *one,*
Alive beyond the Earth and sun.
Spirits *are,* as spirits *do*
And *so,* my love, we rendezvous!

We rendezvous, my love, it's true.
OUR MAKER joined us, me and you.
WE'VE been FREED from mortal dread
By RESURRECTION FROM THE DEAD!

14. This Secret Place, 2/6/25

Highway 27 rest stop north of Perry, Florida

How I love to meet with you
IN this SECRET place of ours!
IT'S a HOLY rendezvous
Beyond the realm of days and hours.
LIVE with ME in heaven, dear.
It's SO much BETTER way up here!
PRETTY as it IS, down there,
There's FAR MORE, dear, up HERE, to SHARE.

Share with me, my heav'nly bride,
The secrets of that lovely land—
That land they call the "Other Side."
Help me, dear, to understand
How it is we live like this,
Sharing Earthly/heav'nly bliss!
Can it be, I've died with you,
To share this special rendezvous?

Yes, my dear, you KNOW it's TRUE—
That fateful day, you DIED with me.
HOW else COULD we rendezvous
And taste this heav'nly ecstasy?
WE could NEVER part, my dear.
Death, himself, can't interfere!
How I love to meet with you,
HERE—and THERE in Timbuktu!

15. We Grow Closer, 2/6/25

A séance poem

Darling, I'M in LOVE with YOU!
DON'T you THINK I'm NOT!
Remember wedding number two—
Our wedding vows are not for naught.
I'M not DEAD and GONE, my love,
FAR REMOVED from you above!

More entwined, we grow, my love,
With *every passing day.*
I know *what* I'm ***speaking of,***
For, *I* can *feel* your heav'nly sway.
Far away, I know, you're NOT—
Our wedding vows are not for naught.

Don't believe I'm more remote
With EVERY PASSING DAY.
Here, above, I love to gloat,
You and I have found our way.
WE grow CLOSER, bumblebee,
Gliding through eternity.

16. Peace and Joy and Love, 2/7/25

A morning poem

Peace, I share with you, my love—
The peace that's stronger than the grave—
The peace that's gentle as a dove—
The peace that makes you wise and brave—
Wise and brave, to live your life,
Triumphant over grief and strife.
Peace, I share with you, today,
To help you, dear, along your way.

Joy, I share with you, dear beau—
The joy that makes us ONE in life—
The joy that causes me to crow:
"Forever, we are man and wife!"
Joy is yours and mine, to share,
All your days, my dear, down there.
Joy, God gives to you and me
That lasts for all eternity.

Peace and joy and love are ours—
Ours, forever, bumblebee!
While you count the days and hours,
Stronger, grows our unity.
ONE, we are, in life and death,
Sharing, even now, your breath.
I will live within you, dear,
Until you're done with month and year.

17. Today and Yesterday, 2/7/25

Enjoy our life of YESTERDAY.
Enjoy our life TODAY, as well.
Living now in heaven's sway,
In past and present, we can dwell.

Reminisce, and you will see
The past is ours TODAY, my love.
The past is more than reverie.
The past is here with us, above.

TODAY, my love, and YESTERDAY
Presume to be like you and me.
Joined, as one, they romp and play,
Delighting in eternity.

I am with you yesterday—
Today, *as well, dear Earthly beau.*
Though you're robed in Earthly clay,
To and fro, my dear, we go.

18. Especially at Three, 2/8/25

At 3 a.m., my dear,
Yesterday is clear.
At 3 a.m., I see
The joy of *You and Me.*
Yesterday, at 3 a.m.,
Shines—a perfect gem.

Heaven shines, at three,
My dear, for you and me.
EARLY, go to bed,
To dine on heav'nly bread.
At 3 a.m., my Earthly man,
YESTERDAY, we live again.

To and fro, we go,
At 3 a.m., below.
A special glow, we know,
Where heav'nly breezes blow.
When the *sun* is *gone,*
We *meet* in heaven's dawn.

YESTERDAY is clear,
At 3 a.m., my dear,
For, HEAVEN SHINES more BRIGHT,
Providing second sight.
Rendezvous, with me,
Especially at three!

19. Sealed, 2/8/25

Sealed until the day I die—
Sealed, my dear, are you and I!
Sealed, as one, while yet we live
This life that only God can give.

Glory, dear, in ME AND YOU!
Let's rejoice to rendezvous!
Our Maker sealed us till that day
You CAST AWAY your Earthly clay.

Heaven, on Earth, is ours, today,
Though I'm robed, dear, still in clay.
God is able, yes, my dear,
To seal us till I'm through, down here.

WHEN the Reaper does you in,
THEN, my dear, will WE BEGIN
The life our Maker sealed us for—
The life beyond that Earthly shore.

20. The Other Me

Charles Santiago, 2/8/25

"Forget me not," means *this,* to me—
We *didn't,* darling, cease to be.
"Forget me not. Forget me not"—
Means *this*—Our love is not for naught.
Love is stronger than the grave
And teaches death how *to* behave.
Death must grant to lovers, all,
Life beyond the mortal fall.

How could *I* forget you, dear,
When, lo, I've found that *you're still here?*
Forget it, darling, *I* won't *be*
Forgetful, *ever,* of unity.
Even when I touch my skin,
I'm aware we *still* are kin.
"Forget me not?" Oh, *no,* my love—
You're the *other me,* above.

21. Feel Our Union, 2/9/25

Feel me, darling, breathe IN YOU—
It proves that we are ONE, not TWO.
Place your hands upon your breast—
Feel, IN YOU, our heav'nly rest.
Listen to the lack of noise—
Glory in our heav'nly poise!
*I am **you**, and **you** are **me**—*
God has blessed our unity.
WE are ONE, much more, today,
*Than **when** I **faced** that Earthly fray.*
We're ONE, in life. We're ONE, in death.
Feel our union in your breath.
Now, my love, go back to sleep.
A vigil, over you, I'll keep.

22. A Gift, 2/10/25

I believe these *words I love.*
They're a *gift* from God above!
I will *never* let them go
While I travel here, below.
Words I love direct me to
The life I share, above, with you.
Words I love can also show
How, within me, dear, you glow.
What a *link,* these words, my dear—
Joining you to me, down here!

Joining you to me, up here,
WORDS YOU LOVE, indeed, are dear!
The alphabet, until you die,
Will serve us as a heav'nly tie.
These WORDS YOU LOVE, on Earth, can shine,
Displaying how two souls entwine—
Entwine, my love, beyond the tomb,
Remaining, yet, a bride and groom.
*Dear Earthly beau, I **love** them **too**—*
These words connecting me and you!

23. More and More, It's Clear, 2/10/25

Johnny Vaughn memorial bench
Kanapaha Botanical Gardens
Gainesville, Florida

More and more, it's clear, my dear—
You *didn't* go *away*.
More and more, I *feel* you *here*,
Abiding *in* my *clay*.
Oh, what joy, to walk with you!
Oh, what joy, to rendezvous!

Oh, what joy, to rendezvous
With YOU, my EARTHLY beau!
WE could NEVER BE just TWO.
We're DESTINED, dear, to grow—
To grow, TODAY, dear bumblebee,
Beyond an Earthly reverie.

To grow beyond this Earthly dream—
Oh, *yes*—I *feel* it's *so!*
Things are *not*, dear, *as* they *seem*—
We *travel* to and fro.
You descend in*to* my *clay,*
And *I* ascend to **heaven's day!**

Ascend, my love. Ascend today.
MAKE our JOY complete!
Leave, behind, your Earthly clay.
In heaven, take your seat!
More and more, it's clear, my dear—
Our union didn't disappear!

24. Earthly/Heavenly Bliss, 2/10/25

Memorial gazebo for Nick and Alexis Posey
Kanapaha Botanical Gardens
Gainesville, Florida

Believe it's true. Believe it's true!
*I am **here**, my dear, with you!*
Why believe your Earthly eyes,
So PRONE to FEED you Earthly lies?
"Your loved one lost her flesh and SO—
AWAY, to heaven, she did go!"
Don't believe it, bumblebee!
Close your eyes and see it's ME—
ME, with YOU, right HERE, right NOW,
THOUGH you CAN'T explain just HOW.
Life, my dear, is SO much MORE
Than JUST a FLING on EARTH'S dirt FLOOR.
HAVE we RENDEZVOUSED, so long,
For you to think we don't belong—
Don't belong, dear Earthly beau,
Side by side, down here, below?
*I **protest**, dear. I **protest**!*
Sweetheart, DON'T be LIKE the REST!
DEAD AND GONE is just a lie,
To hide, from men, the by-and-by.
*I am **here**, right **by** your **side**,*
Your faithful, ever-loving bride.
Believe the eyes within your soul—
Today, we STILL make UP one WHOLE.
The by-and-by, for us, is THIS—
Sharing Earthly/heav'nly bliss.

25. Heaven's Sway

Charles Santiago, 2/11/25

Thoughts on yesterday's trip to
Kanapaha Botanical Gardens
Gainesville, Florida

When you said, dear, yesterday,
"*A trip, let's take, dear bumblebee—
Let us move, to heaven's sway,
Enjoying myst'ries of YOU AND ME,*"
I complied with joy, my dear,
Always game to feel you near.
Heaven's sway is *such* a *thrill,*
Dispensing *with* Earth's *gloomy* chill!

It never fails—this rendezvous—
To thrill, dear, in the core of me,
The core of me that's *Me and You,*
Joined, *today,* in ecstasy.
"*To Gainesville, let us drive, today,
To thrill, my dear, in heaven's sway.*"
So, you *said*—and, *so,* we *went*—
Off, to Gainesville, heaven-sent.

"*A garden's just the perfect place*"
(Gainesville words you said, before)
"*For US to tarry, face-to-face.*"
I agree—But, dear, there's more!
While we tarry, thrilled by grace,
I escape, dear, time and space!
Trips, below, in Night and Day,
Move us, dear, to heaven's sway!

26. I Confess to Know, 2/11/25

How I love to rendezvous,
Every day, my dear, with you!
I confess to know it's true—
Dear, our union isn't through.

Morning, noon, and night, I know,
We are sharing heaven's glow.
You did *not* depart—Oh, no!
In the spirit, I feel us grow.

Every night I go to bed,
Less and less, do *I* feel **dread**.
More and more, I feel, instead,
Resurrection from the dead!

Resurrection, dear, is key
In understanding YOU AND ME.
Because I'm risen, bumblebee,
You, yourself, from death, are free!

27. Prove, to Me, You Fear No Dread, 2/12/25

A morning poem

Death is not a tragic end.
Death, my dear, can be a friend.
HAVE we NOT found, YOU and I,
DEAD AND GONE is just a lie?
WE would lie, were WE to say,
*All I **was**, was merely clay.*
I'M so GLAD you KNOW it's TRUE.
Because you DO, we rendezvous.

Heaven, dear, for me, is THIS—
To walk, with you, in wedded bliss.
Love, my dear, would be remiss
If, after death, we couldn't kiss.
A kiss, for us, is so sublime,
It rescues you from space and time!
WE have learned, dear bumblebee,
How to, STILL, be YOU AND ME!

*I **say** these **things** again, my dear,*
*To prove I **didn't** disappear.*
YOU can FEEL me when I speak
Because, my dear, our love, you seek.
Before you rise, now, from your bed,
Prove, to me, you fear no dread—
LAUGH, my busy bumblebee,
And walk, this day, down there, with me!

28. Another World, 2/13/25, full moon

Inspired by the 1932 film *Smiling Through* starring Norma Shearer, Leslie Howard, and Fredric March

In confidence, my dear, abide—
No matter, that your body dies.
LIKE two SWANS, today, we glide,
In rapture, far beyond Earth skies.
Of course, my dear, by now, you know,
YOU are NOT that BODY—NO!
Confidence in God's dear love
Has brought you to our home above.

Beyond a doubt, my dear, I know,
Our love is stronger than the grave.
I can *feel*, today, we grow.
Like *belle* and *beau*, we still behave.
Even *now*, before I die,
We're *walking* in the by-and-by.
In confidence, I now abide,
One, with you, my heav'nly bride.

ONE, with you, my Earthly beau,
I abide, your heav'nly bride.
WE are ONE because we know,
It's JUST the BODY, dear, that died.
Another world, my dear, we've found,
While YET you TARRY on the ground.
Recall—We NEVER said goodbye.
This love we share could never die!

29. Traveling, 2/14/25

A Valentine's Day poem

Every day, I know it's true—
Our Maker, dear, has brought us here.
God has joined us—*one,* from *two.*
Our union cannot disappear.

Here we are in Timbuktu—
You and I, dear Earthly beau.
Here we are in heaven, too,
Beyond the reach of mortal woe.

When we died, dear heav'nly belle,
Wedding bells, the angels, rang.
Things, for us, have turned out well
Despite a fleeting, mortal pang.

Every day, I know it's true—
You and I were meant to be
Joined as ONE, and never TWO,
Traveling through eternity.

30. Like Two Swans, 2/14/25

A Valetine's Day séance poem

Heaven, dear, for you and me,
Until your final Earthly day,
Is learning, more and more, to see,
WE are ONE, dear, COME WHAT MAY.
Our life, below, my Earthly beau,
Will be a life in which WE GROW,
Closer, closer, bumblebee,
Until our wedding number three!

WE have learned, quite well, my dear,
This lovely art of rendezvous.
I will **never** disappear—
Let's enjoy, dear, Timbuktu!
Enchanted, let us both respond
To mountain, valley, stream, and pond.
Then, when done with month and year,
Like two swans, we'll glide up here!

31. Years and Years Ago, 2/15/25

Inspired by "Love's Been Good to Me" sung by Frank Sinatra

You cast your net, my heav'nly belle,
Years and years and years ago.
You cast it, sweetheart, oh, so well.
Believe me, dear, I know it's *so*—
For, *I'm* the *one* you caught, my dear,
Years and years ago, down here.

I cast my net, my Earthly beau,
Years and years ago, for YOU.
*I could **tell** that **we** would **glow***
FOREVER, *dear, as ONE—not TWO.*
And SO it IS, dear bumblebee—
We shine, today, as YOU AND ME!

Love's been good to us, my love,
Beyond my power to understand.
Somehow, I *live* with *you,* above.
Two *different worlds,* we've *spanned!*
Hand in hand, my dear, let's go.
Somehow, you *knew* we'd, *ever,* glow.

32. Speechless, 2/16/25

Close your eyes and rise, my dear.
Leave that breathing corpse, below.
Let the moonlight make it clear—
I'm your belle, and you're my beau.
Rise beyond that lovely moon.
NOW'S our special time to spoon.
Kiss me, darling, on my lips.
Place your hands upon my hips.

Oh, what rapture, dear, is ours,
Beyond the moon, beyond the sun!
Freed from months and days and hours,
Now we really CAN be ONE!
Isn't it romantic, dear,
Meeting THERE and meeting HERE?
What a lovely rendezvous—
Spooning, NOW, as ME AND YOU!

Speechless, sweetheart, *here,* am I—
Though *fond* of words, I can't reply.

33. Our Special Zone, 2/17/25

A sunbathing poem

Are we closer, dear, today,
Than we *ever* were before?
Don't you feel my heav'nly sway?
Can't you feel "forevermore?"

Do you really live, down here,
Within the *very* soul of me?
What a question, dear, so queer!
Are we not a unity?

Then, my dear, I'm *not* alone—
All *by myself* in Timbuktu?
Dear, you're in our special zone—
"YOU ARE ME, AND I AM YOU!"

Will you be, dear, by my side—
Let's *see*, let's *say*—in fifteen years?
I'M your EVERLASTING bride!
Darling, vanquish all your fears!

I'm so glad we rendezvous,
Side by side, and hand in hand!
Sweetheart, we are, never, TWO—
Two DIFFERENT WORLDS, today, we've spanned!

34. Love Abounds, 2/18/25

WHEN my body died, my love,
*WE fit **MORE** like hand in glove.*
IT'S because you understand
WE can LIVE in such a land.
You believe, my dear, we CAN,
And SO, my love, we live again.

Our lovely creed describes this life
Of Earthly man and heav'nly wife.
What a *life* it *is,* my dear—
Living *there* and living *here!*
It seems, sometimes, it *just* can't *be,*
But *then,* I feel our ecstasy!

Mind to mind, and soul to soul,
YOU can feel we STILL are whole.
Even in your body, dear,
YOU can TELL I still am near.
Trust your hunches, bumblebee—
Let them lead you, here, to me.

Heaven knows that *we* are *one*
Beyond and underneath the sun.
How it works, I *just* can't *tell,*
But *we* remain, dear, beau and belle.
I believe our Maker can
Grant us, now, to live again.

Love, my darling, conquers death.
Love abounds beyond mere breath.
This truth informs our ecstasy:
*"I AM **YOU**, AND **YOU** ARE **ME**."*
Clasp my hand, my Earthly beau.
Beyond mere Earthly life, we'll go!

35. Romantic Movies, 2/18/25

Inspired by the film *Golddiggers of 1935* starring
Dick Powell, Gloria Stuart, Alice Brady, and Adolphe Menjou

Stalk me, darling, *all* you want.
All your heav'nly powers, flaunt.
At the ready, dear, I stand
To meet you in that other land.
Heaven is—*this rendezvous!*
Well I've learned, my dear, it's *true.*
Come to *me.* I'll *come* to *you*—
There's *nothing,* dear, I'd rather do!

Watching movies is a link.
Watch and, dear, you'll SEE me WINK.
Romantic movies, bumblebee,
Are JUST the THING for you and me.
Our love, my dear, can never die.
Even WAITING is JUST a LIE.
Romantic movies lift us high,
WAY up, TO the by-and-by.

Death is not a separation.
Really, it's emancipation.
WE are FREED, my love, today,
To walk in heaven's lovely sway.
Romantic movies, bumblebee,
Open doors for you and me—
Doors allowing us to see
Heaven is—our unity.

36. Wedding Bells Are Ringing, 2/19/25

Remember wedding number one.
Reminisce with me, my dear.
Joining hands beneath the sun,
WE began our journey HERE.
WE were thrilled at OUR ROMANCE.
WE were joined, dear, NOT by CHANCE!
GOD had YOU in mind for me
Before I called you "bumblebee."

Remember wedding number two—
How it took us BY SURPRISE.
You, my dear, thought WE were THROUGH!
YOU were FOOLED by death's disguise.
Death, you thought, had done us in—
YOU were DRUNK with Earthly gin.
I'M so GLAD, dear Earthly beau,
Our heav'nly ties, you came to know.

WHAT a GIFT for me and you—
This rendezvous that now is ours,
Thanks to wedding number two
And help from mighty, heav'nly powers.
Rendezvous with me, my love,
Until you're due to come above.
Wedding number three awaits,
Here, inside of heaven's gates!

Indeed, it's true, dear heav'nly bride—
God had *me* in *mind* for *you*.
Like two swans, in heaven, we glide,
In *this*, our lovely rendezvous.
You were *meant* for me, as well—
You're my everlasting belle.
Wedding bells are ringing, dear.
I can *hear* them, way down here!

37. Via Highway 27, 2/19/25

A morning poem

Let us rendezvous, this day.
I am ***game****,* dear. *I* am ***game!***
Life on Earth is *so* passé
Unless, this rendezvous, we claim.
Claim me, *dear,* and *I'll* claim *you.*
How I love to rendezvous!

I'VE been WAITING, bumblebee,
To see you stir from slumber, THERE.
I'll WALK on EARTH, today, as ME,
For, YOU'RE the Earthly clothes I wear.
Start the car. Let's GO to HEAVEN
Via Highway 27!

I can't ***wait*** to start the car
To take a day trip, here, with you!
Heaven, dear, is where you are—
Like *in* the *car* in Timbuktu.
Our ride down Highway 27
Will *surely* be a trip to heaven!

38. There's a Lot That I Can Do! 2/19/25

Inspired by "Just as Though You Were Here" sung by Frank Sinatra

Wacissa River Park
Wacissa, Florida

Every day, remember THIS—
ALL does NOT depend on you!
My love for you, dear, don't dismiss.
There's a lot that I can do!
*I can **wake** you up and say,*
"Let's go for a ride today.
Highway 27, love,
Beckons us to soar above."

In the details of your life,
"Way down there," in Timbuktu,
*I can **be** your doting wife,*
Always walking next to you.
Sweetheart, please believe it's SO!
Do not doubt our heav'nly glow!
*I can **hear** each word you say—*
I'M not GONE, my man of clay!

Death is not a separation—
Not for those like you and me.
We've been touched by RESURRECTION.
Life beyond the grave, we see!
Romantic love—this gift of ours—
Is helped along by heav'nly powers.
Take to heart, my words to you:
*"**There's a lot that I can do!**"*

39. Death Is Not a Separation!

Charles Santiago, 2/20/25

How I love to hear the phrase:
"Death is not a separation!"
We've begun a brand-new phase
Spurred by *this,* dear—*resurrection!*
Raised from bodies made of clay,
Spirits, heaven's light, display.
Death did not destroy our life.
Death confirmed us, man and wife.

"Death is not a separation!"—
Music, darling, to my ears!
Death, instead, is *celebration*—
We've been *freed* of mortal fears!
We can live beyond the Earth,
Sated with sweet heaven's mirth!
I can tell these things are true
Because of *this,* dear—*I* know *you!*

Death is not a separation!
Spirits *are,* as spirits *do.*
We are joined in exultation.
Spirits, dear—We rendezvous!
Heaven came to you and me,
That awesome day of liberty.
Freed from clay, you clasped my hand,
And now we live in heaven's land.

40. A Clever Rhyme, 2/21/25

A morning poem

Shine, my dear, the truth of US
By means of THIS—a clever rhyme.
Rhyme, with holy zeal, and THUS,
Share with me this love, sublime.
Rhymes reflect this holy glow
You and I have come to know.

This holy glow we've come to know
Is nestled, dear, within my breast.
The rhymes we pen are all aglow
With joy and peace because we're blessed
With union, here and now,
That angels help allow.

Doors were opened to heaven, above,
At wedding number two.
You and I now share this love
Beyond mere Timbuktu.
I believe we'll rhyme, my dear,
Until, from Earth, I disappear!

41. Our Mortal Scar, 2/22/25

WE are learning how to fly
Beyond the bounds of Earth and sun.
BINDING, is this lovely tie,
Preserving us, today, as ONE.
Everywhere you go, my dear,
*Chant your phrase, "I **know** she's **here**!"*
*I **know**, my love, you **know** it's **true**—*
*I have **not** deserted **you**!*

Regardless, dear, of WHERE you ARE,
Regardless, dear, of WHAT you DO,
Remember that our mortal scar
*Is proof that **I** belong to **you**.*
*I am **yours**, and **you** are **mine**,*
BY our Maker's grand design.
AS the Earth goes round the sun,
WE continue being ONE.

AS you trek through night and day,
*I keep **walking** next to you.*
When, at last, you're done with clay,
Still, my dear, we'll rendezvous.
WE have learned to live beyond
Mountain, valley, stream, and pond.
Beyond the Earth, beyond the sun,
Life, for us, has now begun.

42. I Believe in Resurrection! 2/23/25

I believe you're ***here***, my love,
More than *I* can realize.
I believe I'm ***there***, above,
With *you*, my love, my heav'nly prize.
I believe in resurrection!
I believe in celebration!
I believe we're *one*, right now—
To our *union*, death must bow!

I believe I died with you,
More than I can realize.
I believe our rendezvous
Proves our union never dies.
Everlasting love, I see,
God is giving you and me.
It's ***almost*** more than *I* can ***bear***—
To feel we live both *here* and *there!*

Live your life, my dear, IN ME,
Beyond that lowly Timbuktu.
God has granted us, our plea—
To live, TODAY, as ME AND YOU!
Heaven is—THIS LIFE WE SHARE,
Way up here and way down there.
Everlasting love, you said,
Would trounce the kingdom of the dead.

YOU were RIGHT, dear bumblebee—
Death could not destroy our bond!
*I am **you**, and **you** are **me**,*
***There**—and in the great beyond.*
While, my dear, you're robed in clay,
Enjoy, with me, this heav'nly day.
WHEN you're DONE with Earth and sun,
WE'LL continue being ONE!

43. So Much More than Clay! 2/24/25

What a great dishonor, dear,
To say that you're, no longer, here!
Heavens! What a cad I'd be—
To say that you deserted me!
It would be a *sin,* I'd say,
To *think* you *went* so *far* away,
So *far* away that *we* were *through*—
Through, my darling, me and you!

"All alone, am I, my dear,
Now that you're, no longer, here!
Far away, you flew, my love,
Way, way, *way* up *there,* above!
There's no *way* that *we* could *be,*
Still, together, you and me!"
—Words, my dear, of unbelief,
Designed to fill me full of grief!

"Remember, dear, that day I died,
And, in our union, you'll abide."
SO, I've said, to you, my beau,
To help you slay that wicked foe—
That wicked foe of all mankind,
Who's placed, so many, in a bind.
Speak, my darling, from your heart—
Could we EVER be APART?

Never, dear, could you and I
Say our love could *ever* die!
Death is just for those who think
God can *not* provide a link.
There's no end to *Me and You—*
Spirits *are,* as spirits *do.*
We rejoice, my dear, to say:
"*We* are *so* much *more* than *clay!*"

44. Harmonize with Me, 2/24/25

*Am I **here**, or **am** I **not**?*
Did we not, dear, tie the knot?
Are you SURE, my Earthly man,
You and I can live again?

Oh, how sweet to be in love
There, below, and here, above!
Oh, how sweet, my dear, to be
ONE with you, in harmony!

Harmonize with me, each day,
As the angels show the way.
Our Maker, dear, is calling us
To ride this lovely, heav'nly bus!

*Yes, I'm **here**, and **I** will **be***
Yours for all eternity.
I'M so GLAD we tied the knot—
SEE, my dear, what God has wrought!

45. These Words You Love, 2/25/25

Read and write these words you love,
All your days down there, below.
THEY will LEAD you here, above,
To meet with me, dear Earthly beau.
These words you love can help you, dear,
To find our lovely home, up here.

This corpse that's mine, down here below,
To its Earthly grave, descends.
*While it's **headed** for its woe,*
Your Earthly beau, to heaven, ascends.
*I can **tell**, these words of ours*
Align my soul with heav'nly powers.

Angels guide you, bumblebee,
On your trek through Timbuktu.
To help you find your way to me,
WORDS you LOVE, they give to you.
These WORDS you LOVE, dear, READ and WRITE,
And everything will turn out right!

46. Laugh, My Earthly Man! 2/26/25

Close your eyes and think of me,
And then, my love, BELIEVE.
Believe in THIS, dear bumblebee—
*I could **never** leave!*
Death cannot destroy our bond.
Love is like a magic wand.
WHEN the body bites the dust,
Lovers spoon, as lovers MUST.

MUST you think that death is real?
Have more faith, my love!
Don't deny, dear, what we feel—
*A **new** life **here**, "above."*
Close your eyes, dear. Close your eyes—
Believe in life above Earth skies.
While you trek through Timbuktu,
Life is still, dear, ME AND YOU.

I'M so PROUD of you, my dear.
YOU believe it's TRUE—
YOU can LIVE with ME, up HERE
*While **I** live **there** with **you**.*
Laugh, oh, laugh, my Earthly man—
GOD says WE can live again!
Clasp my hand, and I'll clasp yours.
Rejoice with me—Our love endures!

47. We Taught Death How to Behave, 2/26/25

A morning poem

You chose me, and I chose you,
Long ago, dear heav'nly bride.
Never, would we say adieu
Even though your body died.
Oh, what joy I feel, today,
Joined with you in heaven's sway!
We taught *death* how *to* behave—
Love is stronger than the grave!

*I chose **you**, dear Earthly beau,*
Way down there in Timbuktu.
Then I left our home, below,
UP HERE, with you, to rendezvous.
To and fro, we've learned to fly,
Preventing, dear, a sad goodbye.
Our Maker showed us how to grow
Beyond that dismal world of woe.

48. A Higher Way, 2/27/25

WE are SPIRITS, AND we KNOW
Bodies come and bodies go.
Earth and sun, and night and day,
Lead us to a higher way.

A higher way, my dear, we've found
Though your body's on the ground.
Night and day, we rendezvous
ABOVE—and THERE in Timbuktu.

In Timbuktu, we came to know,
IN HEAVEN, we were meant to grow.
Night and day have led us to
This life, my dear, that IS our DUE—

Our due because our Maker said:
"Come and eat this heav'nly bread—
RESURRECTION FROM THE DEAD—
Freeing you from mortal dread."

From mortal dread, we've BEEN set FREE—
Free, my darling, free to be
Alive beyond the land and sea,
Enjoying, NOW, eternity.

Eternity has called us, dear,
Free to be, of mortal fear—
Free to be, to disappear
From night and day, and month and year.

49. Month by Month, 2/27/25

67th month anniversary of wedding number two
A séance poem

Month by month, time *creeps* along,
As, my dear, I slowly die.
Something, sweetheart, *seems* so *wrong*,
Here, below Earth's lovely sky.
How can time, dear, pass so *slow*
Even though, the Truth, I KNOW?
It *seems* so *long* ago, my dear—
That *day* I *saw* you disappear!

Close your eyes and think of me.
Induce, my dear, a holy trance.
***YOU** should KNOW, dear bumblebee,*
The awesome POW'R of OUR romance!
COUNTING DAYS, my Earthly beau,
Makes you feel like time goes slow.
Count, instead, the many times
WE find HEAVEN through our rhymes.

50. Walking in Eternity, 2/28/25

Sit, my dear, and let us rest.
LET'S consider HOW we're BLESSED.
Angels open doors for us,
Allowing us, dear, to discuss
WHAT a joy it is to be
Walking in eternity.
What JOY it IS to grow our love
There, below, and here, above!
YOU'RE my special valentine—
I'M so BLESSED to call you mine!
Take my hand, dear Earthly beau.
*I am **yours**, from head to toe!*

God has been so good to us,
Freeing us from Matter's fuss.
Soaring, dear! We're *soaring,* dear—
Soaring past my mortal fear.
I can *feel* our home, above,
Far beyond Man's *push* and *shove*.
Peace, my dear, is ours, today.
How I love our heav'nly sway!
You're still *you.* I *know* it *well.*
You *dwell* in *me,* dear. *I* can **tell**.
I am **thrilled** that we can be
Walking in eternity!

51. Soon Enough, 3/1/25

A sunbathing poem

Though it *may* seem *strange* to *some*,
It means *everything* to *me*,
To feel you, to your temple, come,
And prove to me that we can be
Alive and well, my heav'nly belle,
Together, here on Earth, to dwell.
How I love to live with you
In heaven—*and* in Timbuktu!

All your days on Earth, below,
YOU will BE my temple, dear.
Day and night, you'll feel my glow
Until, from Earth, you disappear.
Do not worry, bumblebee.
Darling, you're the OTHER ME!
WE cannot be split, in two.
WE are ONE, dear, through and through.

Be patient, dear, for I am *still*
Robed in garments made of clay.
How I wish that I could *will*
To be *beyond* Earth's dreary sway!
God has willed us, HERE, to be
An Earthly He and heav'nly She.
Enjoy, my dear, this rendezvous.
Soon enough, will IT be THROUGH!

52. Two Temples

Charles Santiago, 3/2/25

Of this house, dear, let me speak—
This house that's built of brick and wood.
Since you "left," it's *so* unique.
This *house* can *make* me *feel* so *good!*
This house has now become a place
Where *you* and *I* speak, face-to-face.
Really, dear, you're living here
In this house. It's very clear.

Of this house, dear, let me speak—
This house that is uniquely *me.*
Every day of every week
Since you "left," I feel so free,
Free of life's impending doom—
A "resting place" within a tomb.
There's a certain heav'nly glow
That, in my body, now, I know.

Two temples, I've discovered, dear,
In my *trek* through Timbuktu.
How I love to feel you near
In these lovely temples, two!
Double pleasure, dear, is ours
In this *realm* of days and hours.
In this *body* and *in* this *house,*
We rejoice, as man and spouse.

53. We Adhere

Charles Santiago, 3/2/25
A sunbathing poem

The reason I exist, my dear,
Is *this,* my darling—We adhere.
I have **learned,** these Earthly eyes
Feed me naught but Earthly lies.
I can *see* through death's disguise
And meet with you, *below* Earth skies.
I'm a temple—Yes, it's true.
Here, on Earth, we rendezvous.

Our fate, my dear, has always been
This life we're sharing, deep within.
Our Earthly bodies come and go
While *you* and *I,* true **union,** know.
What peace it brings, in Night and Day,
To feel, my dear, your heav'nly sway!
Praise Almighty God, above,
For *this,* our everlasting love!

54. Our Union, 3/3/25

Let your body die, my love.
Let your body die.
YOU'VE a home with me, above.
Our union doesn't lie.
Our union lies beyond your breath—
Beyond the land of so-called "death."
Our union, dear, is ALL THERE IS—
He is hers, and she is his.

AS the Earth goes round the sun,
All your days below,
WE'LL continue being ONE
In HEAVEN'S lovely glow.
Hand in hand, dear, hand in hand,
WE enjoy this lovely land.
Let your body die, each day,
AS we MOVE to heaven's sway.

Live your life, dear Earthly beau,
Conscious of our tie.
Feel, my dear, our heav'nly glow—
Our union doesn't die.
I'm GRATEFUL FOR this LIFE we SHARE,
Way up here and way down there.
AS your body dies, my dear,
GREATER, is our life, up here.

55. Our Special Time, 3/3/25

A séance poem

Sunset, dear—that holy time—
Is *just* when *I* should pen a rhyme.
Goose bumps, on my neck, reveal,
Yes, our union *still* is real!

COME to ME. I'll COME to YOU
WHEN the daylight hours are through.
NOW'S our special time, my love,
To rendezvous up here, above!

Empowered by our holy love,
I can *feel* our home above.
Resurrection, dear, is true,
Bringing joy to me and you.

You have *come,* and *I* can *tell,*
Dear, we *fit* together *well.*
Dead and Gone is so untrue—
I *know* because, dear, *I* know *you!*

All those thirty years, on Earth,
Have brought, to you and me, this mirth.
Darling, I will walk with you
Until you're done with Timbuktu.

56. Reach for Heaven, 3/4/25

Reach for heaven, every day.
Live beyond the earth and sea.
Darling, you are more than clay—
YOU'RE a part of YOU AND ME.
WE have found this Shangri-la
Filled with peace and joy and awe.
Realize, dear Earthly beau,
YOU can UP, to heaven, go!

How I love to walk with you
As you reach for heaven, above.
Our life below, in Timbuktu,
Should make you think, dear, "hand in glove."
What a perfect combination—
YOU and ME, a new creation!
WE'VE been made anew, my dear,
No longer, bound by day and year.

Live, my darling, filled with peace.
WE'RE released from Earth and sun.
Soon enough, your breath will cease,
But, **NOW***, our* **NEW** *life* **HAS** *begun.*
Day and night, I live, in you,
Till day and night, my dear, are through.
Reach for heaven, every day.
Dear, I'm with you all the way!

57. Come Aboard! 3/4/25

Inspired by the film *Romeo and Juliet* (1936)
Starring Norma Shearer and Leslie Howard

How cruel to think that I, my dear,
Would live apart from you, down there!
How sad to think that death could jeer:
*"I **broke** their **union** beyond repair!"*
*I was **not** that body—no!*
From your side, I didn't go.
MORE than Earthly clay, are we—
We can still, a couple, be.

Our Maker, dear, intends for us
To live together, still, as ONE.
Come aboard this heav'nly bus.
Leave, behind, the Earth and sun.
Entwine, my dear, entwine with me.
Our home is in eternity.
Our loving Maker calls us to
Live together, me and you.

WHEN we died, my Earthly beau—
Died to life in Timbuktu—
GOD gave US this heav'nly glow,
Tailored JUST for me and you.
See, my dear, how WE have GROWN
Beyond the need for you to groan?
Our Maker, dear, is leading us
Beyond the mire of mortal fuss.

58. Let Me Know You See, 3/5/25

Grin, my darling bumblebee.
Grin and let me know you see
Death is unreality.
THIS is real, dear—YOU AND ME.

Smile, my darling Earthly man.
Smile because you know "We CAN"
Sport a lovely, heav'nly tan,
All because we live again.

Laugh—Oh, laugh, my Earthly groom!
WE'RE all THROUGH with Earthly gloom!
Our love can now, in heaven, bloom,
Far beyond an Earthly tomb!

59. I'm Beside You, 3/5/25

A séance poem

Bumblebee, I'll corner you
To make you see we're ONE, not TWO.
Believe it, darling, if you dare—
I'M beside you, everywhere.
I'm aware—Believe it's SO—
Of all you do, dear Earthly beau.
Don't lose out. Oh, don't lose out
By caving in, my dear, to doubt!

BELIEVE it—I'M not GONE AWAY!
BELIEVE it, all the livelong day!
*EVERY MOMENT, I am **there**.*
Your VERY soul, my dear, I share.
God is giving THIS to US—
Freedom from Earth's mortal fuss.
Take it, please, my dear, from me—
You and I, from death, are free!

60. This Special Life, 3/6/25

I have ***found*** that you can be
Alive and here, my dear, with me.
Far more *than* I *realize,*
We have *won* a heav'nly prize.

I have found that we, my love,
Share a life that's here, above.
Our Maker means, for us, to know
This special life of belle and beau.

Come, my darling, clasp my hand.
Meet me in this heav'nly land.
*I will **walk**, below, with you*
THERE, my dear, in Timbuktu.

Hand in hand, dear, you and I
Will share this lovely by-and-by.
I'm content to live and die,
Enjoying heaven, on the sly.

61. Quite a Love Affair! 3/7/25

That day my body died, my dear,
Began this life we share, up here.
*I am **proud**, my dear, **of you***
For learning how to rendezvous.
God has proved, to you and me,
Love is for eternity.

I believe that God can give,
To you and me, this life we live.
Though our flesh became unpaired,
*Lo, we live because we've **dared**—*
***Dared** believe that you and I*
Are more than bodies, here, that die.

*I can **feel** our life, above,*
Though I'm dwelling here, below.
God has given us this love
Of heav'nly belle and Earthly beau.
Angels, guide us, here, I pray,
Until my final Earthly day.

ONE LIFE, we share because we dare
Believe our love can never die.
Ours is QUITE a love affair,
Unfolding THERE, beneath the sky.
How I love to live with you
Until your days, my dear, are through!

62. Row Your Boat, 3/7/25

A séance poem

I can *feel*, dear heav'nly bride,
We have spanned the Great Divide.
By our Maker's love and grace,
Darling, we speak, face-to-face.

ONE, we ARE, dear Earthly beau,
Enjoying heaven's lovely glow.
WE don't need the Earth and sun—
Our heav'nly life has, now, begun.

Intertwined, are we, my love.
I know **what** I'm **speaking of**.
Your arms, around me, I can feel—
So *real* and yet, dear, *so* surreal.

Row your boat, my Earthly man—
Row your boat, dear, down the stream.
WE have found, we LIVE AGAIN,
And, mind you, dear—It's NOT a dream!

63. Just a Scar, 3/8/25

Our mortal wound, I see, today,
Is *just a scar,* and *I abide*
Beyond the grave, and far away
From *thoughts,* my dear, that *you* have *died.*
Our mortal wound *has healed,* I see,
And *we remain,* dear, He and She.
Earthly bodies, *we* don't *need,*
The law of love, my dear, to heed.

Heed, my dear, that law of love—
That law of love by which we live.
Thou, below, and I, above,
Live this life that God can give.
The law of love has banished death,
And now we live beyond your breath.
Our mortal wound, my Earthly man,
Is JUST A SCAR—We live again!

64. A New Creation, 3/9/25

When I went to heaven, dear,
THEN it WAS, I entered you.
Though it sound a little queer,
THAT explains our rendezvous.
WITHIN you, darling, I abide,
And YOU, in heaven, now reside.
WHILE your body walks the Earth,
WE are joined in heav'nly mirth.

A new creation, dear, are we!
WE are free of day and night.
WE are free from earth and sea—
Free, my love, of mortal fright!
Though your body, THERE, must die,
WE can tour the by-and-by!
Live below and live above,
Joined with me in heav'nly love!

Hand in hand, dear Earthly beau,
God allows us, now, to be!
AS we travel to and fro,
Rejoice, my love, in YOU AND ME!
I proclaim my love for you
THERE, below, in Timbuktu.
I proclaim, dear, YOU are MINE—
My eternal valentine!

65. *Read* These Words! 3/9/25

A séance poem

READ, my dear. Don't merely WRITE!
READ these words you love so much.
Through the day and through the night,
These words can help us keep in touch.
This Earthly/heav'nly repartee
Keeps us smiling, on our way.
Don't neglect to READ, dear beau,
These rhymes that shine with heaven's glow.

These *words I love* are quite a link.
They *thrill* me *through* and *through!*
They're like a heav'nly rum I drink
That *brings* me *close* to *you.*
How I love to write these rhymes
That usher in such heav'nly times!
But *read* them, *dear,* I *will,*
And *rest,* a *while,* the *quill.*

66. All Is Well

Charles Santiago, 3/10/25

Dear heav'nly bride, I must profess
The wonder of that sacredness—
That sacredness revealed by you,
On Earth, at wedding number two.

Angels, in their fine array,
Came, as servants, on that day.
I could *feel* their holy power
In your final Earthly hour.

You were ready, my heav'nly bride,
To travel to that Other Side.
You were strong, and you were brave,
Knowing you'd escape the grave.

I can *feel,* today, my love,
Your sacred presence in heaven above;
For, *I'm* a *temple* in *which* you *dwell,*
And I profess that *all is well.*

67. Fly! 3/10/25

Inspired by the music "Offerings" by Bryan Carrigan (and by the young girl swinging gleefully from the swing-rope over the water)

Wacissa River Park
Wacissa, Florida

Fly, sweetheart. Fly—
Fly beyond mere Timbuktu.
Fly so high
You bid adieu
To mountain, valley, stream, and pond,
And THERE, my darling, we'll respond
To God who made us ONE
THERE, below, beneath the sun.
And WE'LL rejoice that WE are FREE—
FREE to touch eternity.
Then, my darling, fall back down,
And I'LL DESCEND with YOU,
Wearing, dear, my heav'nly gown.
And, when your Earthly days are through,
Beyond Earth sorrows, we'll rendezvous.

68. Wicked Earthly Eyes, 3/11/25

A sunbathing poem

DEAD AND GONE—No, DON'T BELIEVE IT!
Not EVEN, DEAR, for JUST a LITTLE bit!
EVERLASTING, is our love,
Abiding, dear, up here, above.
Live a THOUSAND years, my dear!
Our union cannot disappear!
Oh, those WICKED Earthly eyes—
How they LOVE to feed you lies!
Sweetheart, I'M not LEAVING YOU!
How could we, my love, be through?
Read and write our lovely rhymes,
To share, with me, dear, heav'nly times.
But KNOW, dear BEAU, that THIS is SO—
Without one rhyme, we STILL will grow.
FOREVER, God has set us free
From DEAD AND GONE and misery!

69. Our Life's Not Through! 3/11/25

A séance poem

How I love to remember you
Because I know our life's not through!
"Forget me not," I know means *this*—
We are sharing heaven's bliss.
It seems like *yesterday*, my dear,
We were holding hands, down here.
What *joy* it *is*, today, to be
Still, my darling, *You and Me!*

DEATH could NOT split US, in TWO!
Death has proved our love is true!
YOU did NOT forget me, dear.
FAR from THAT, you JOIN me HERE!
YOU did NOT forget that we
FOREVER, would be YOU AND ME.
"Forget me not," I said to you,
Not knowing of this rendezvous!

You have not forgotten *me!*
We've maintained our unity!
How could we have known, my love,
You'd *still* be *here*—while *there, above?*
Dead and Gone, I thought was true,
Dear, at wedding number two!
We have found the love we crave—
Life beyond the gloomy grave!

70. Here, Below, 3/12/25

A sunbathing poem

I am *understanding,* dear,
More and more, that *you* are *here.*
Heavens! Life on Earth can be
Ecstasy for you and me!
Death, O Death, you *can* not *bring*
Misery—You *have* no *sting!*
We have *found* the Promised Land
By walking *here,* dear, hand in hand!

PEACE, my darling, PEACE is ours,
HERE, below, in days and hours.
Heaven gives to me and you
This Earthly/heav'nly rendezvous.
YOU have LEARNED to catch my drift.
Darling, what a heav'nly gift!
TILL your DAYS on Earth are through,
I'll be walking HERE with you.

How I love this point of view:
"Spirits *are,* as spirits *do.*"
We can *walk* on Earth, below,
Sharing heaven's lovely glow.
We can *fly* beyond the sun
Holding hands, my cherished one!
I am *you,* and *you* are *me.*
Life, my dear, is ecstasy!

71. I'm Trailing You! 3/13/25

Listen, dear, and YOU will HEAR.
LOOK—and YOU will SEE—
I'm not gone, dear. I am HERE.
YOU'RE the OTHER ME.
*I can **work** through time and space*
To meet you, face-to-face!

Dear, you're not the only one!
I'M ALIVE and WELL!
My love for you is not undone—
*In your **soul**, I **dwell**.*
Every day, I'm trailing you
UNTIL your DAYS are THROUGH!

Without a form that you can see,
*I am **by** your **side**.*
How I love this mystery—
*I am **still** your **bride**!*
Believe it, dear! Believe it's true—
*I can **live** with **you**!*

72. Increase Awareness, 3/13/25

Increase awareness, bumblebee—
Awareness, there below, OF ME.
"YOU'RE the other ME," I say.
"I'M the other YOU," today.
Sweetheart, I'm not far away!
Consider me WITHIN YOUR CLAY!
ONE, we ARE, TODAY—It's true.
*I **dwell**, my **love**, inside of you!*
WE don't HAVE to WAIT, dear beau,
To share in heaven's lovely glow.

Stretch your mind. Oh, stretch your mind!
TO my PRESENCE, don't be blind!
Be aware that I'M not LESS!
I'M still ME, dear, I confess.
I can see you tie your shoes.
I can see you watch the news.
WHEN you STAND in LINE, I'm THERE.
*I am **with** you **everywhere**.*
Increase awareness, dear, I pray,
And we'll go on our merry way!

73. Joined Today, *As One*, 3/14/25

A séance poem

I'M abiding, dear, in you.
I'M so GLAD you know it's true!
*I still **live** in Timbuktu*
Because our union's never through.

You and I, my dear, are free
To glory in this ecstasy—
This ecstasy of YOU AND ME,
Enjoying, NOW, eternity!

FREEDOM, dear, is ours today—
Freedom from that Earthly fray—
Freedom from your mortal clay!
Only BODIES, dear, decay.

We are joined today, AS ONE,
Beholden NOT, to Earth and sun.
Sun and Earth, dear, we can shun.
A home, in heaven, we have won!

74. *Happy*, Be! 3/15/25

HAPPY, be, dear bumblebee!
We are free, dear. We are free—
Free from Earth and moon and sun.
Heaven, for us, has NOW begun!
"YOU are ME, and I am YOU"
Is proof, these things, my dear, are true.
Read, each day, our lovely creed—
That creed, BY DEATH, we came to heed!
—That creed that feeds us, now, this bread:
RESURRECTION FROM THE DEAD!
YOU were THERE, dear Earthly beau,
That day we conquered Adam's foe.
Dear, you THOUGHT that WE were THROUGH!
But WE have LEARNED to rendezvous!
HAPPY, be! Oh, HAPPY, be—
Soon, comes wedding number three!

75. An Earthly/Heavenly Mystery, 3/16/25

Darling, how I love to feel
The beauty of your heav'nly glow!
Resurrection power is real—
It's a truth that now we know.
From your body, you arose,
And cast aside all Earthly woes.
I bear **witness** that it's true
Because, today, we rendezvous.

Rendezvous with me, my love,
Until your Earthly days are through!
Rise, oh, rise up HERE, above.
Leave your clay in Timbuktu.
Share, with me, this heav'nly glow—
*IT'S for **ME**—and **YOU**, my beau!*
Intertwined, as one, are we.
We can share this ecstasy.

Till my Earthly days are through,
This will *be* true *life* for *me*—
Life together, dear, with you,
An Earthly/heav'nly mystery.
Dance with me, my beau, oh, dance!
We've been saved by our romance!
WHAT a DAY in Timbuktu—
That day we said, my dear, "I do!"

76. *Bodies,* We Don't Need, 3/16/25

Highway 27 rest stop north of Perry, Florida

A body, sweetheart, *I* don't ***need;***
Neither, dear, our lovely creed.
Just *our union,* beyond my clay,
Rescues me from Earth's dismay.
Let this body die or live,
We enjoy what *God* can *give.*

God can give this life we share—
But YES, my dear, because WE DARE.
*I love **you**, and **you** love **me***
Sufficient for eternity.
BODIES, we don't need, my dear.
Earthly bodies disappear.

Appear UP HERE, dear Earthly beau.
How our Maker loves us SO!
Our Maker gives, to you and me,
Life beyond Earth's reverie.
Let your body live or die—
Our home is here, beyond the sky.

77. Heaven's Lovely Glow, 3/17/25

Death, my dear, has taught me *this*—
Lovers never say goodbye.
Even when I reminisce,
I can *feel* our heav'nly tie.
This makes lovers truly brave—
"*Love is stronger than the grave.*"

WE have DARED believe, my dear,
Our love is stronger than the grave—
Stronger than Man's mortal fear
That tries, Man's spirit, to enslave.
We are freed from death, dear beau,
Because of heaven's lovely glow.

78. When *You* Embraced Me, 3/18/25

*When **you** embraced me **when** I **died**,*
THEN, began this rendezvous.
Now, my dear, we BOTH reside
Beyond the bounds of Timbuktu.
A new creation, we became.
Things can never be the same.
Timbuktu could never be
A home that's fit for you and me.

Night and Day, dear, JUST won't DO!
Earthly clay is SO passé!
WE'RE a different ME AND YOU.
Don't you feel bright HEAVEN'S DAY?
Day and week and month and year—
Let them, darling, disappear.
Hand in hand, let's soar beyond
Mountain, valley, stream, and pond!

Remember, dear. Remember me,
Every moment there, below.
A heav'nly couple, dear, are we,
Meant, in heaven, now to glow.
Eat and drink, and work and sleep,
Our rendezvous, my dear, to keep.
When YOU embraced me, bumblebee,
THEN, began this ecstasy.

79. This Love Affair, 3/18/25

A sunbathing poem

This life we're sharing, bumblebee,
*Cannot die. It **WILL** not die.*
Our Maker made us, you and me,
Eternally, a girl and guy.
I profess my love for you
HERE—and THERE, in Timbuktu.
*I **do**. I **do**, dear Earthly beau,*
Cherish you from head to toe!

Likewise, darling, I profess,
You're my *one* and *only* love.
You are *all* my happiness,
And *I* know *what* I'm ***speaking*** of—
I was ***there***, dear. *I* was ***there***
When ***you*** and ***I*** began to dare
Believe that we could *never* be
Split apart, dear, you and me.

That day when we began to dare
Believe that we could live anew,
Began, my dear, this love affair,
This Earthly/heav'nly rendezvous.
Our love survived the mortal blow
Endured by lovers, linked below.
Death has proved, to you and me,
Our love is for eternity.

80. Just a Passing Phase

Charles Santiago, 3/19/25

I won't ***die***. I ***know*** it's ***so***
Though this body ***surely*** will.
When this body dies, below,
To ***heaven's glory***, I will thrill.
Death is just a way for me
To leap into eternity.
Who I ***am*** is ***so*** much more
Than ***things*** I ***feel*** on ***Earth's*** dirt ***floor***.

I will ***thrill*** to life anew—
Life anew beyond my skin!
I will ***have*** a lovely view
From my ***room*** in Heaven's Inn.
Life beyond my skin is real
Though ***here***, below, it ***seems surreal***.
My, how foolish it would be
To think there was ***an end*** to me!

Sometimes, here below, I feel
I'm in ***heaven***, now, today!
I declare! It feels so ***real***—
This joy I feel outside my clay!
This Earthly clay in which I dwell—
This place to which dear Adam fell—
Is just a passing phase I'm in
On my ***way*** to Heaven's Inn.

81. By Our Maker, We Are Known, 3/19/25

I am *not* myself alone!
I am *you,* dear. *I* am *you*!
By our Maker, *we* are *known,*
Who *made* us *one,* dear, out of *two.*
I would *lie,* dear. I would *lie*—
To say we ever said goodbye.

I am you, dear Earthly beau!
I am you, dear, through and through!
Of course, my darling, IT is SO.
God has made us ME AND YOU.
*We will EVER, **EVER**, be*
This union, sweetheart, YOU AND ME.

82. A Sun Beyond, 3/19/25

A sunbathing poem

Use the sun and use the night,
Resurrection rhymes, to write.
I'm alive, my dear, IN YOU,
THOUGH, with day and night, I'm THROUGH.

Close your eyes and go beyond
Mountain, valley, stream, and pond.
Wedding number two means THIS—
WE'RE not BOUND to EARTHLY bliss.

Like we've said, dear Earthly beau,
Bodies come, and bodies go.
Spirits ARE, as spirits DO—
And so, my dear, we rendezvous.

There's a sun beyond the ken
Of those who never shout "Amen!"
Bask in HEAVEN'S lovely sun.
LIFE for US, dear, HAS begun!

I'M not RESTING in a grave!
*I have **found** the love I crave—*
Life with YOU, the OTHER ME,
The one I christened "Bumblebee!"

83. Clasp My Hand, 3/20/25

Don't believe your Earthly eyes.
Believe, my dear, in heav'nly ties.
Don't believe I've passed away.
Believe, instead, in heaven's day.
Will you doubt this rendezvous
Heaven's giving me and you?
Will you doubt our vows, my love,
Joining us, up here, above?

Let that body pass away.
YOU are NOT that body—no!
YOU'RE much MORE, my dear, than clay!
Let that Earthly body go!
Clasp my hand in Timbuktu
And bid, to Earthly clay, adieu.
Enter, dear, into our love
Shining here, in heaven, above.

84. To Love, *Today*, 3/20/25

A sunbathing poem
First day of spring

AT THE READY, be, dear beau,
At the start of every day.
All your plans, the angels know.
THEY can HELP us FIND our WAY.
How they love to see us meet—
In our pew, to take our seat!
They are experts, bumblebee,
In helping souls like you and me.

EXPECT it, dear, to be this way.
Heaven LOVES, dear, YOU AND ME!
On the lookout, be, each day.
THEY will HELP us. YOU will SEE.
Be prepared, my Earthly man,
For you and me to live again.
There's no need for us to WAIT!
To love, TODAY, dear, is our fate!

85. Without or With, 3/21/25

Without or with these words you love,
We'll commune, dear Earthly beau.
Way down THERE or HERE, above,
On our way, my dear, we'll go.
Without or with a body, dear,
TO each OTHER, we adhere.
Our Maker made us, ONE, to be—
I am you, and you are me.

Without or with the sun and moon,
We will spoon, as lovers do.
Croon, my dear, and I will swoon—
All my ecstasy are YOU!
*A **fine romance**, have you and I,*
Without or with an azure sky.
Rudy Vallée, be, to me.
Mae West, to you, my dear, I'll be.

You're my life, my ecstasy,
Without or with the Earth and sun.
Eternal love has set us free
From being *two*, to being *one*.
Without or with these *words I love*,
Hand in hand, we stroll above.
Rendezvous! Let's rendezvous—
Nothing can, our love, undo.

86. Every Single Day, 3/22/25

DO not PANIC, bumblebee.
I'M not LEAVING YOU.
YOU'RE a TEMPLE, DEAR, for ME
UNTIL your DAYS are THROUGH.
Angels lead us, day and night.
Don't cave in and live in fright.
Continue in this way we've found
Here, above, and on the ground.

WHEN you THINK I'm far away,
YOU are WRONG, my love.
I abide, dear, IN YOUR CLAY
AND up HERE, "above."
Steady as she goes, my dear.
Remember, I am always HERE—
HERE, beside my Earthly beau,
WHEREVER on the Earth you go.

I'M enjoying life with you
Every single day.
Remember, dear, our life's not through!
To THINK like THAT'S PASSÉ.
My, how FAR we've COME, my dear,
SINCE that day, that day, so queer!
I'm so glad that you and I
Never, darling, said goodbye.

87. Every Moment of the Day, 3/22/25

Every day, I wait for you
To waken from your slumbers, dear.
*I can't **wait** to rendezvous*
*And show, to you, how **I am near**.*
*I want **you** to be aware*
***We're** in Hallelujah Square!*
EVERY SECOND, dear, for us,
WE'RE on board this heav'nly bus!

Speak to me, dear bumblebee,
Without or with your Earthly lips.
Set your heav'nly eyes on me!
Place your hands upon my hips!
Don't be blind, my Earthly man—
Every day, we live again!
EVERY MOMENT of the day,
WE can MOVE to heaven's sway!

Walk, with me, on streets of gold
THERE, my dear, in Timbuktu!
YOU can DO it, IF you're BOLD.
*Believe, dear, **that** I **live in you**!*
***Dear, I know** you **know** it's **so**—*
Higher, HIGHER, we can go!
THERE'S no NEED to DIE, my love,
To live with me in heaven, "above."

88. Thank the Angels! 3/22/25

A sunbathing poem

Angels, dear, have got our backs.
ALL does NOT depend on US.
BE all THROUGH with panic attacks!
ANGELS drive this heav'nly bus.
Sit BACK, my dear. Enjoy the ride.
God has, to our pleas, replied.

I have **faith** to **believe** it's **true**—
Love is *stronger than* the *grave!*
You live *here* in Timbuktu.
Our Maker grants this love we crave!
Every second, all day long,
We prove *Dead and Gone* is *wrong.*

DO what you WILL, my Earthly man.
I will ***prove***, *to you, it's true—*
You and I, dear, live again
Until your Earthly days are through.
Thank the angels, if you will.
Angels help us—What a thrill!

89. *Dead and Gone* Is *So* Untrue! 3/23/25

I will *love* you there, above,
All my days, down here, below.
We will *fit,* dear, hand in glove,
Sharing heaven's lovely glow.
Dead and Gone is *so* untrue!
Death, cannot, true love, undo.
From *Earth* and *sun,* dear, *we've* been *freed!*
Earthly bodies, *we* don't *need!*

I will love you there, below,
Until you breathe your final breath.
Hand in hand, we then will go
Beyond that realm that's ruled by death.
We've discovered WE can BE
Linked in heav'nly ecstasy
WHILE you TREK through night and day,
Living out your life of clay.

    Sweetly, do you speak of love—
    One, above, and one, below.
    Walk together, hand in glove,
    As *heav'nly* belle and *Earthly* beau.
    We will *help* you till it's time
    To rise to life that's more sublime.
    The Great Almighty, over all,
    Saves you from dear Adam's fall.

90. A Lovely Mystery, 3/24/25

Come, dear, let us pen, tonight,
Rhymes describing YOU AND ME—
HOW we've learned to take our flight
Into heav'nly ecstasy.

I have *learned* to meet with you,
Here within the depths of me—
Here beyond mere Timbuktu—
Here beyond Earth's reverie.

*I have **learned** to meet with you,*
THERE where deathly breezes blow—
THERE in lowly Timbuktu,
Linked by heaven's lovely glow.
*"I am **you**, and **you** are **me**"*
Is quite a lovely mystery!

91. Because We Are a Unity, 3/24/25

A morning poem

Again, begins a brand-new day—
A brand-new day for *Me and You*.
How this heavy, Earthly clay
Hampers, dear, my heav'nly view!

Close your eyes and think of me,
And HEAVEN WILL come INTO view.
Because we are a unity,
YOU can LIVE in heaven, too.

Also, dear, remember THIS—
Our lovely creed is heaven-sent.
WE can SHARE a blissful kiss
If, TO our CREED, we GIVE ASSENT.
HOW this lovely creed of ours
ENHANCES, dear, our heav'nly powers!

92. This Holy Hush, 3/24/25

A séance poem

This holy hush, again, has come—
This holy hush that thrills me *so!*
I can **hear** a heav'nly hum
Because, my dear, *today,* we grow!

"TODAY, we grow!" Oh, YES, it's SO!
Angels gather, round about!
WE can SHARE in heaven's glow
BECAUSE you've CONQUERED grief and doubt!

I have **learned**, dear heav'nly belle—
To *feel* this hush, I *must* be *sure,*
Sure that you're *alive* and *well,*
Sure our union *can* endure.
When the angels gather near,
We escape, dear, month and year!

93. Death Tried Hard! 3/24/25

A séance poem

How I love to rhyme with you!
Our rhymes reflect this *You and Me*.
I *love* to sit, dear, in our pew,
Rejoicing in our liberty!

Freedom, dear, is ours, today!
Freed, are we, from day and night.
Though you're robed, dear, still in clay,
WE are FREED from mortal fright.

Death tried hard to break our tie,
That fateful day, that day you died.
Even *now* he loves to try
Convincing *me* we *don't* abide—
Don't abide, as *Me and You*,
But, **with** his **lies**, dear, *I* am **through!**

94. Every Moment, 3/25/25

Every moment, yes, my dear,
We abide beyond the sun.
While this body dies, down here,
I can *feel* that *we* are *one!*

God is kind to us, dear beau,
EVERY MOMENT, every day.
Death turned out to be no foe.
Death, our union, couldn't slay!

God, our Maker, gives to us
These words we pen, down here, my love.
And so, by pen, dear, we discuss
The wonder of our life above—
We can move, to heaven's sway,
Every moment, come what may.

95. *Stronger,* Grows Our Love, 3/25/25

Yes, my dear, it's, oh, so TRUE—
WE'VE survived the mortal blow!
Else, we couldn't rendezvous
Or feel this lovely, heav'nly glow.

ENJOY, my dear, this life, above,
THERE, below, in Timbuktu.
WE can savor heaven's love
WHILE, on Earth, we rendezvous.

STRONGER, grows our love, my dear,
Regardless of the Earth and sun.
Earth and sun will disappear—
WE, my dear, will still be ONE!
WE'RE not bound by night and day.
Come, dear, let's be on our way!

96. A Doorway, 3/25/25

A sunbathing poem

Death is just a doorway, dear,
A doorway to a higher way.
Don't regard it, dear, with fear—
It's JUST the DAY you LOSE your CLAY.

Higher, dear, will we ascend,
Higher than we could before.
NO one DYING, will, THEN, DESCEND.
EARTH, dear, IS the BOTTOM FLOOR.

WE'LL continue, you and I,
IN this LOVELY upward climb.
Already, WE have LEARNED to fly—
*The FLIGHT will JUST be **MORE** sublime.*
Rest, relax, and, HAPPY, be!
Angels guide, dear, you and me.

97. I *Remember* You, 3/26/25

I *remember* you, my love.
Then, behold, I *feel* you, dear!
Truly, we walk, hand in glove—
You, up there, and *me*, down here!

MORE than MEM'RIES, dear, have we!
A life that's SHARED—Today, is ours.
Faith and love are always KEY—
BELIEVE, and you'll see heav'nly flowers.

Heav'nly flowers, I send to you—
SIGNS, my dear, that help you see
You and I can rendezvous.
I am **you**, and **you** are **me**.
We are temples, you and I,
Sharing, now, the by-and-by.

98. Yearning for Our Liberty, 3/26/25

A morning poem

You're determined, I can tell,
To prove, to *me,* that *we* can *be*
An Earthly beau and heav'nly belle
Until, from Earthly clay, I'm free.

You KNOW me WELL, dear bumblebee,
For, YOU can TELL I'm THERE, with YOU,
Yearning for our liberty,
At last, my dear, from Timbuktu!

I am determined, yes, it's so,
To prove, to you, that I will be
In love with you, my Earthly beau,
Until your day of liberty.
ONE, in death, and ONE, in life—
Signed, my dear, your loving wife.

99. A World Apart, 3/27/25

WE have found, dear bumblebee,
A world apart from THAT, below.
WHY engage in misery
When WE can sway to heaven's glow?

Heaven found us, dear, THAT DAY.
Angels call us, you and me.
Shun that world in disarray.
Why engage in misery?

Lift your eyes. Oh, lift your eyes,
Earthly beau, to better sights—
Better sights beyond Earth skies,
Beyond those Earthly days and nights.
Why engage in misery,
Neglecting, dear, our liberty?

100. Love That Never Dies! 3/27/25

Inspired by the film *Ziegfeld Girl* (1941) starring Hedy Lamarr, Philip Dorn, Lana Turner, James Stewart, Judy Garland, and Jackie Cooper

Hedy Lamarr, are *you*, to *me*—
Fair and beautiful, yes, indeed!
Philip Dorn, I *long* to *be*,
From *loneliness*, by *you*, dear, *freed!*

Oh, how SWEET, to be in love!
Romance me, darling, through the "veil!"
Rise, from Earth, to heaven above.
Through the heavens, let us sail!

Words I love, dear heav'nly bride,
Speak of love that never dies!
You and I are on a ride,
Trav'ling far beyond Earth skies!

"Love that never dies"—oh, YES—
Our Maker gives to you and me.
WE were MEANT, my dear, I "guess,"
To, EVER, be a unity.
I am yours, *dear Earthly beau.*
Higher, HIGHER, let us go!

101. Lovers Thrill to Unity! 3/27/25

We're aligned, dear. I can tell.
Peace pervades my inmost core.
All is well, dear. All is well.
Death, we've found, was just a door.

Adore our Maker, bumblebee.
Our Maker grants this peace we own.
If, NOW, we LIVE, as YOU AND ME,
NEVER, will we be alone.

One, we *are,* and *one,* we'll *be*
When *gone* are Earth and moon and sun.
Our Maker calls us, you and me,
FOREVER, to be joined, as one.

When, this holy hush, you hear,
Thank our Maker, bumblebee.
Though the body disappear,
Lovers thrill to unity!
It's JUST the BODY, dear, that died.
As groom and bride, we still abide!

102. Abiding in Our Unity, 3/28/25

Now that we have found our place,
In and out of time and space,
Darling, you can rest, at ease,
Having learned your ABCs.

ABCs teach bumblebees
How, indeed, to be at ease.
I can truly *happy*, be,
Abiding in our unity.

"I am you, and you are me"—
Darling *what* a recipe
For peace and joy in Timbuktu,
Walking hand in hand with you!

Walking hand in hand, with you,
In and out of Timbuktu!
Darling, we have found romance,
In and out of Paris, France!
Our Maker gives us WHAT we CRAVE—
Life beyond the ghastly grave!

103. Timbuktu, O Timbuktu! 3/28/25

Delightful, was that *life* we *had.*
But *now,* my dear—It's *not* so *bad!*
Every day, I learn anew,
I'm *not alone,* in Timbuktu.
What a *thrill* it *is,* my dear,
To *feel* your *presence still* down here!

EVER, will it BE, my love,
A **miracle***, up here above,*
Walking hand in hand, with you,
As ONE, my dear, and, never, TWO.
God has made provision for
Life, together, forevermore!

Timbuktu, O Timbuktu!
How I'm *grateful* just for you!
In your realm, I *found* the *one*
With whom I live beyond the sun!
Heavens! We're aligned, my dear,
You, up *there,* and *me,* down here!

104. Let's Meet at End of Day, 3/28/25

A séance poem

FOLLOWING, bumblebee, am I—
FOLLOWING you through Timbuktu.
Death, dear, didn't break our tie!
I am **living there** with **you**!

Sundown is our special time.
Dear, let's meet at end of day.
Don't be guilty of a crime
By clinging to that Earthly clay!

At the ready, be, dear beau,
When the sun goes out of sight.
WE can travel to and fro,
BEST, my dear, when comes the night.

CAN you FEEL me close to you,
MORE, just now, dear bumblebee?
When the sun is out of view,
I can **feel** you **feeling me**!
This holy hush at séance time,
Dear, has spawned this holy rhyme!

105. I Believed, 3/29/25

Now that we have found our life,
Let that body find its grave.
WE'LL behave like man and wife.
God has granted WHAT we CRAVE.

Crave, my darling bumblebee,
Life beyond mere night and day.
Believe in God. Believe in me.
Believe in life beyond Earth's fray.

While you tread that Earth, below,
Clasp my hand in heaven, above.
To my friends, up here, I crow—
You and I have found true love.

Love is stronger than the grave.
You and I have found it's true.
The ghastly grave has made me brave—
Brave enough to rendezvous.
I believed in *You and Me,*
And found, with you, eternity.

106. Graves and Tombs and Pyres, and Such

Charles Santiago, 3/29/25

Heavens! Darling, I have found,
In our *union*, I abide.
I recall that day you died
And feel us both, in heaven, crowned!

Graves and tombs and pyres, and such,
Invite the world to contemplate
A way to get past heaven's gate,
With loved ones, *thus,* to stay in touch.

Death is just an entranceway
To life that's *on* a *higher* plane.
And yet, the "the dead" can still remain
With *loved* ones *who* can feel their sway.

I have *felt* your sway, my dear,
Ever since that fateful day—
That day you left, behind, your clay,
And seemed, my love, to disappear.
We have found, though, you and I,
Communion in the by-and-by.

107. Earthly/Heavenly Ecstasy, 3/29/25

A séance poem

When you *want* to come to me,
Doors and walls can't *keep* you *out!*
Our union is a mystery,
Unknown, my dear, if *there* is *doubt.*

Sweetheart, like we've said before:
"*Bodies, we* don't *need*—oh, no!"
Through this Earthly/heav'nly door,
We *both* can travel to and fro.

"*I* am *you,* and *you* are *me*"—
That's the key, dear, *to* this *door.*
Earthly/heav'nly ecstasy
Thrills me, darling, *to* my *core!*

WHEN the SUN sets IN the WEST,
Oh, my darling, come to me!
Join me in this holy quest
Of union in eternity!
A séance, dear, between us two,
Is proof, indeed, our love is true!

108. Love Has Saved Us, 3/30/25

Love has saved us, bumblebee—
Saved us from the ghastly grave.
What a lovely mystery—
To die—and find this love we crave!

I'm content, dear Earthly beau—
Content to clasp your hand and be
Filled with heaven's lovely glow,
Rejoicing in our unity!

YOU'RE my lovely Earthly man.
Our Maker, dear, has made us ONE!
Glory, dear! We live AGAIN,
Basking under HEAVEN'S sun!

Love has saved us. Yes, it's true—
Saved us, dear, from night and day.
Our Maker made us *one,* from *two,*
While, as yet, we *lived* in clay.
Heavens! *How* God *loves* us *so*—
To grant, today, this life we know!

109. ABCs, 3/31/25

Don't despise the ABCs.
Remember, though, dear Earthly beau—
ABCs, for bumblebees,
Stem from heaven's lovely glow.

Don't neglect your ABCs.
Read them often, bumblebee.
*Remember how I **like** to **tease**.*
ABCs can show you—ME.

Beyond the ABCs, my dear,
Looms our home on heaven's shore.
ABCs can bring you HERE
For RESPITE FROM that LOVELY WAR.

Arm yourself with ABCs.
Read and write them. Know them WELL.
ABCs can help you seize
Knowledge THAT will HELP you dwell
IN our HOME on heaven's shore,
Happy, dear, forevermore.

110. All We Need, 4/1/25

Darling, we have all we need
Until your Earthly days are through—
The creed, BY DEATH, we came to heed,
And YOU ARE ME, AND I AM YOU.

Our union was not shattered by
Eden's snake, Man's wily foe.
After, dear, you HAD your CRY,
We LEARNED to WALK in heaven's glow.

"WALK with ME. I'll WALK with YOU."
Has brought us now to streets of gold.
That lovely law of rendezvous
Has made us fearless, made us bold.

Night and Day is SO passé!
A higher life, dear, we demand.
Since I left, behind, my clay,
The gulf between two worlds, we've spanned.
Darling, we have all we need.
Let's proceed, dear. Let's proceed!

111. Believe in Love, 4/2/25

Don't be silly! Believe in love.
Believe in life beyond your skin.
WE are DESTINED to FLY above
Earthly Man's preposterous din!

Don't be silly! Believe IN ME!
Believe in me—THE OTHER YOU!
*Believe me, darling, I can't **be**,*
WITH your EARTHLY body, through!

Believe, my dear—TODAY, we're ONE.
BODIES, WE don't NEED—oh, no!
WE'VE been FREED from Earth and sun
***Since** I **left** my clay below.*

Believe in life beyond your skin.
Could our union cease to be?
Darling, you're my closest kin.
INDEED, you ARE—THE OTHER ME!
Don't be silly, my Earthly man,
And THINK we COULDN'T LIVE AGAIN!

112. Our Bold Romance, 4/2/25

Because of grief, because of pain,
To die, on Earth, is heav'nly gain.
Believe, my dear, in life above—
Above Man's vicious push and shove.

Believe, dear beau, in WORDS I LOVE,
Streaming from this life above.
When, my love, you breathe your last,
Grief and pain will, all, be passed.

Pass, with me, a life of joy.
DEAR, I'll BE your Myrna Loy.
William Powell, dear, BE to ME.
Our bold romance will set us FREE—

FREE from Earthly day and night,
FREE from mortal pain and fright,
FREE to live, forevermore,
Far beyond that Earthly floor.

113. Resurrection Love, 4/2/25

Wacissa River Park
Wacissa, Florida

Let's proceed, dear. Let's proceed
To write, each day, this lovely creed—
This creed of vict'ry over death—
Of life beyond mere human breath.
Oh, my dear, let's go beyond
Mountain, valley, stream, and pond.
WE know WHAT we're SPEAKING of—
WE know RESURRECTION LOVE!
My body died but, dear, you know
We share, today, in heaven's glow.
Death tried hard to MAKE you THINK
That flesh, my dear, was ALL our link.
But, BY your FAITH in ME AND YOU,
Today, my love, we live anew!
Your faith, dear, SAVED us FROM the grave!
YOU refused to BE death's SLAVE!
Continuity is ours
Beyond the realm of days and hours.
God's GIFT to US, as man and wife,
Is THIS, my dear—eternal life!
Let that body pass away—
That body, dear, that's made of clay.
LET'S now LIVE in heaven's day—
Far beyond that mortal fray!

114. Going Our Way, 4/3/25

WE'VE discovered, bumblebee,
Heaven, guiding you and me.
"Put your nets out HERE," they say—
Angels who are going our way.
GOING OUR WAY, dear! Angels who
Know about our rendezvous!

I'VE discovered, oh, my love,
WE'RE alive in heaven, above!
WE'RE alive—in spite of death
Robbing you of Earthly breath!
Heaven came to you and me
To help us sail this heav'nly sea.

Steady as she goes, my love.
Heaven's guiding you above.
While you sail through seas, below,
EVERLASTING LOVE, we know.
*I am **thrilled** to sail with you*
On seas, below, in Timbuktu!

Sail with me! Come, *sail* with *me*
On our ship named "Liberty."
Heavens! Darling, *I* have ***found***,
You and I, in heaven, are crowned!
Angels who are going our way
Free us from Earth's disarray!

115. "It," 4/3/25

MORE than you KNOW, dear bumblebee,
*I am **living** there with you.*
*I still **claim** you, dear, for **me**,*
*And, **no**, my love, I **don't** say "Boo!"*

Peace and love are ours, today.
LIKE we've SAID, "We need not wait."
Angels, yes, are going our way,
Helping us to celebrate.

WHEN you HEAR that holy hush,
Angels, dear, are helping us.
So, TAKE it EASY. Dear, don't RUSH!
Free yourself from Earthly fuss.

Romantic love, today, is ours.
YOU'RE my GUY, and I'M your GIRL.
Pick, for me, my dear, some flowers.
Make my mind go all awhirl!
***You** have "It," like Clara Bow.*
HAND IN HAND, my dear, we'll go.

116. *Today,* We Live! 4/3/25

A séance poem

Read and write, dear. Read and write.
ABCs can, sometimes, be
The way to leave, behind, the night
And taste of heaven's ecstasy.
Oh, what joy our creed can give,
Proving that, TODAY, we live!

We live, my dear. We live, today,
In and out of time and space.
YOU can JUMP outside your clay
And speak to me, dear, face-to-face.
Believe** these **words** which **I** have **said:
"I'M not GONE, and I'M not DEAD!"

Doors and walls can't KEEP me OUT.
*I abide **within** you, dear.*
Listen—YOU won't HEAR me SHOUT.
THERE'S no NEED to SHOUT. I'm HERE—
HERE, like always, bumblebee,
Enjoying, with you, eternity.

117. This Life of Liberty, 4/4/25

Darling, I'm alive—It's true.
Remember, though, my Earthly beau—
I'M alive IN YOU
UNTIL your LIFE is THROUGH.

DEAD AND GONE is SO not SO!
Remember, dear. I'm ALWAYS HERE.
Our MAKER CAN BESTOW,
On US, this HEAV'NLY GLOW.

Dear, I'll never disappear.
Remember me—and ecstasy.
FEEL me, oh, so NEAR,
THOUGH the WORLD may SNEER.

*I have **claimed** you, bumblebee.*
Remember death who stole my breath.
DEATH gave YOU and ME
This life of liberty.

118. I'm Content, 4/4/25

A séance poem

I *have* our *love* for *all* my *life*—
For *all* my *life* in Timbuktu.
Our love dispels all Earthly strife.
What a thrill to walk with you!

"WALK with ME. I'll WALK with YOU"—
The law of rendezvous, my love,
Has KEPT us ONE, in Timbuktu,
And IN our HOME, up here, above.

Darling, I'm content to be
Alive, down here, on good old Earth.
Feeling you, alive in me,
Assures me of our heav'nly worth.

Our union, dear, is ALL MY LIFE—
ALL MY LIFE—Of course, it's SO!
It's GOD who made us man and wife,
IN God's LOVE, to, EVER, grow.
I'M content, my dear, to be
ALIVE with YOU, the OTHER ME!

119. We Still Are *One!* 4/5/25

Rejoice! Rejoice, dear bumblebee!
Heaven's guiding you and me.
You and I can, HAPPY, be,
Having found this ecstasy—

This ecstasy of ME AND YOU,
Living, now, this rendezvous.
Death has served his noxious brew,
And, DEAR, we've FOUND our LIFE'S not THROUGH!

Eve and Adam, dear, are we—
In spite of death, a unity!
WE'VE discovered Eden's tree
Bearing fruit of liberty—

Liberty from Earth and sun!
Heav'nly life has now begun!
*I have **finished** out my run—*
And, lo, my dear, we still are ONE!

120. When It's Time, 4/5/25

WHEN it's time "to go," my dear,
Be prepared, dear. Be prepared!
WHEN it's time to come "up here,"
Remember, THERE, the things we've shared.
WE have shared ETERNAL LIFE
There, on Earth, as man and wife!

WHEN it's time to leave, behind,
Earthly clay, well-known by you,
DO not THINK you're in a bind.
Take your seat, here, in our pew.
Be prepared, dear bumblebee,
To say goodbye to land and sea!

WHEN it's time, oh, WHEN IT'S TIME,
WE will BE prepared, my love,
To pen a rhyme that's SO sublime,
BY its LIGHT, we'll soar above—
Above, at last, my Earthly man,
To don a lovely, heav'nly tan!

www.ingramcontent.com/pod-product-compliance
Lightning Source LLC
LaVergne TN
LVHW051131080426
835510LV00018B/2346